How to Deliver Powerful Presentations

A Step by Step Guide to Improving Your Presentation Skills

By Meir Liraz

Published by BizMove
www.bizmove.com

Table of Contents

MEIR LIRAZ

1. Presentation Objective

Part of every manager's time is devoted to the presentation of plans or ideas. In this chapter we will delve in some detail into how this can be done effectively.

Ralph C. Smedley once said, "A speech without a specific purpose is like a journey without a destination." The first step in preparing a presentation is to establish a purpose or an objective. What is to be accomplished by the presentation? After this has been determined, necessary steps can be taken to support it, and guidelines established to organize it. If the presentation is logically organized by subject matter at the start, it will do much to assure success of the presentation.

A presentation is made to provide information, give instruction, sell a plan or idea, or accomplish a combination of these things. Through words and visual aids, a presentation performs a service to the listener. A carefully worded presentation can translate facts, trends, or statistics into basic relationships that will influence policy or actions.

Rudyard Kipling has said that "Words are the most powerful drug used by mankind." After the objective of the presentation has been established, the general form of the presentation must be considered. The message should be communicated in as few words and using as few visual aids as necessary to present a plan or idea effectively. A concise, convincing presentation of 10-minutes' duration may accomplish readily the desired objective - and be more economical - than one lasting an hour. In other words, the effectiveness of the presentation depends more upon the soundness of the message than its length, the presenter's skill in delivery, or the quality of the visual aids. However, too long a presentation, lack of skill in its delivery, and/or poor visual aids could spell disaster.

2. Presentation Strategy

Once the objective has been established the next step is planning the presentation strategy. The answers to some basic questions will help in this process:

(1) What are you selling?

(2) To whom are you selling it?

(3) Against what are you competing?

(4) In what environment do you expect the message to be received?

What are you selling? Why are you making the presentation? Take another look at the objective. Are you selling a plan of action, a need for action, a product, a service, or support for an idea? Pinpoint the reason for making the presentation. Express it in as few words as possible. John Witherspoon once said: "Never rise to speak until you have something to say, and when you have said it, cease."

To whom are you selling it? If you know your audience, you have some idea of its position on the subject. A presentation that is highly successful before one audience can be a failure before another one. The presentation strategy should be attuned to the audience. Can the people in the audience make a final decision, or must they take your recommendations to a higher authority? Before the presentation, know as much as possible about the people in your audience - their thought patterns, interests, authority, and even their emotional needs. Do they prefer a certain type of visual aid, a break during the presentation, or coffee service? Is their time limited? Remember, people in the audience will have different likes and dislikes. C. W. Spalding, put it this way: "People differ. Some object to the fan dancer and others to the fan."

Against what are you competing? When you know the emotional needs of your audience, the message can be geared to the listener's viewpoint. The benefits to the listener can be targeted. In making presentations, the most common barriers en- countered will be:

• Fear on the part of the listener that the plan or idea may curtail his/her prestige, authority, or prospects for advancement;

• Unwillingness of the listener to undertake something new because it may involve an organizational dislocation or cause a personal irritation;

• Unwillingness of the listener to leave the "beaten" path and/or a hesitancy to stick out his/her neck; and

• The vanity of the listener.

In what environment do you expect the message to be received? There are a number of questions that might be raised to determine the environment in which the presentation will be given. Some of the basic questions are:

• Will the audience be friendly or hostile, sympathetic or unsympathetic?

• Will the audience be open- or close-minded?

• Will you have supporters, or opposition?

• If there is opposition, will it hold a unified or divided opinion?

There are some other factors that tend to affect the success of the presentation, namely:

• When will the presentation be given: early in the morning, after lunch, just before the close of the work day, or after dinner?

• Will the people in the audience be in a hurry?

• Are you "on the spot" for any reason?

• Do you have to save someone's face?

In the final analysis, the strategy you formulate as a presenter should be based upon a knowledge of what you are selling, to whom you are selling it, the barriers you will be encountering, and the atmosphere in which the presentation will be given.

3. Presentation Organization

A successful presentation contains more than good material and the most convincing arguments. It displays good organization of subject matter. The most forceful and persuasive presenter may fail to have a plan, idea, or information accepted by the audience if the message is not organized well.

The introduction and conclusion cannot be neglected. At the outset, the presentation should gain the interest of the audience and convey to the listeners what is to be covered.

In the conclusion, the presenter should review the key points of the presentation and pinpoint the action to be taken, if any.

The body of the presentation, located between the introduction and the conclusion, contains the bulk of the message. It should be presented to the listener in a meaningful form. An outpouring of plans, ideas, or information without form or relationship will not hold the attention of any audience very long.

Organization of the presentation involves fitting the parts into a coherent whole. The method depends upon the subject matter to be presented and the strategy to be used. The most familiar form of presentation is probably the time-sequenced-chronological-approach. The problem-solution pattern is a logical choice for many "in- house" presentations. When there is a need to compare alternative solutions to a problem, the comparison-contrast approach is a good choice.

In an informative presentation, a cause-effect technique might be used. When the purpose of the presentation is to clarify or explain the meaning or nature of something, the definition technique is appropriate. Another form commonly used involves discussing the "parts" comprising the whole, such as subdivision of an organization, or subsystem for components of a missile. Related to this technique is the presentation built around systems, and functions qualities-sub-systems of an aircraft, functions of units within an organization. If the material to be used does not fit into one of the commonly used organizing patterns, the presenter should establish a pattern of his/her own.

When one has an outstanding point to make in a presentation, it should be made normally at the beginning. This has an advantage over "building up" to the main point. If it "sells" the plan or idea, the balance of the presentation then involves "nailing down" the plan or idea. Another reason for leading off with the main point, or points, is that important listeners could be called away before the presenter is finished. If they are, they will not miss the main point.

After a plan or an idea has been sold by citing its major advantage, or advantages the balance of the presentation should generally be treated as reinforcement of that plan or idea. The points to be made should be presented in descending order of importance. Remember, when the main point fails to deliver the message, the lesser points will not do it! Speaking of ensuring the message comes through clearly, I am reminded of the 10-year-old explaining the plot of "My Fair Lady" to her younger sister. She said, "It's about a dirty girl who gets remedial reading."

A presentation should be long enough to accomplish the objective. Generally, a presentation of less than one hour is best. Most audiences don't absorb too many thoughts at a single sitting. Three or four important points can usually be established firmly. On some occasions, a half dozen points can be made if they are very closely related. Supplementary information should be screened from the subject matter before the presentation is made. Such material can be provided as a hand-out, if it is deemed important enough to convey to the audience.

At the end of the presentation, the audience should be left with a memorable impression of what the presenter said; accordingly, the presenter should recap the main point or points. If the presenter is expecting some action after the presentation, he/she should tell the people in the audience what is expected.

A good speaker rehearses his speeches; he practices what he preaches. After the presentation material has been assembled and organized, an evaluation should be made. This evaluation should include consideration of the factual contents as well as the personal delivery. There is always a possibility that someone in the audience will assume a "so what?" attitude. It is advisable to have a personally selected evaluator state what is clear, what is effective, and what should be reworked or eliminated. Undergoing such an evaluation by a friendly "so what" can be likened to seeing a dentist - it is not a pleasant thing to do because it may reveal some trouble, but it could be dangerous not to do so.

Someone has said that want of study, and want of knowing what one is driving at, must bear the blame of many a long and weary presentation. Hence, a short talk is usually of a better quality than a long one, and if it is not, it is all the better that it is short.

4. Presentation Delivery

At the outset, the presenter must establish a rapport with the audience. There must be a flow of understanding and mutual respect between presenter and audience. At the start, the presenter should win the kind of attention needed for the rest of the presentation. His/her walk, posture, facial expressions, hand movements, and clothing will be observed by the audience. Early in the presentation, the presenter will be judged, favorable or un-favorably, by the audience. After the audience decides whether it likes the presenter, it will determine whether it can give credence to what the presenter has to say. One story goes that after giving what he considered a stirring, fact-filled campaign speech, the candidate looked at his audience and confidently asked, "Now, any questions?"

"Yes," came a voice from the rear, "Who else is running?"

To be successful - assuming the message is good - the presenter must be animated, alert, and free from obvious tensions. A simple, indirect, natural, and relaxed style will gain audience acceptance, as will use of variety in voice, body movements, and subject content. The presenter must be intimately acquainted with the principal points and the sequence in which they are to be given, so rehearsals are a must. If the presenter wants to "look alive" to the audience, he/she must know the subject, have an intense belief in the subject, confidence in his/her ability to communicate, and an eagerness to communicate effectively.

The power of words was expressed well in a Look magazine editorial several years ago. Speaking of words, the editorial said, "They sing. They hurt. They teach. They sanctify. They were mar's first immeasurable feat of magic. They liberated us from ignorance and our barbarous past. For without marvelous scribbles which build letters into words, words into sentences, sentences into systems and sciences and creeds, man would be forever confined to the self-isolated prison of the cuttlefish or the chimpanzee."

When words alone fail to present the message clearly, visual aids become an important part of the delivery. Visual aids can help to isolate ideas and clarify problems or relationships. They can also be very helpful when figures are involved or trends have to be conveyed. In many cases, the audience can grasp a plan, idea, or situation more quickly than when the message is conveyed verbally without benefit or aids.

When words will suffice, visual aids should not be used. Dallas Williams questions whether one picture is worth a thousand words as has been sometimes stated. Williams says: "...Give me 1000 words and I can have the Lord's Prayer,   the 23rd Psalm, the Hippocratic Oath a sonnet by Shakespeare, the Preamble to the Constitution, Lincoln's Gettysburg Address, and enough left over for just about all of the Boy Scout Oath and I wouldn't trade them to you for any picture on earth." Unfortunately, a presenter can't put all of these immortal words together to convey a single coherent message. Therefore, carefully planned visual aids are often helpful and effective in conveying messages to a variety of audiences.

5. Some Final Thoughts

The cost of a presentation should be justified, unless the presentation has been directed by higher authority and no alternative is possible. If it has not been specifically directed, the cost of preparing and delivering a presentation must be weighed against the value of the objective to be accomplished. The cost of the time required of the listeners also should be considered.

In weighing alternatives, one might ask, "Can the story be told more economically - and, possibly, as effectively - by an inter-office/ inter-agency memo, letter, meeting in the office, or a telephone call? Finally, let's run down the list of things that you, as a presenter, should remember when you face the audience:

• Speak up. Make yourself heard.

• Keep your back to the wall.

• Avoid any mention of time during the opening comments.

• Watch the faces of those in your audience. Maintain "eye-to-eye" contact.

• Stand erect and control your nervous habits. Don't fuss with your clothes or use annoying gestures.

• Avoid competing with outside disturbances.

• Relax and smile. Avoid smoking.

• Use stories to make your points.

• Reaffirm your points at the end of the presentation.

Now, you should be ready to prepare and make an effective presentation. Best wishes for success in the next one.

MEIR LIRAZ

MEIR LIRAZ

www.ingramcontent.com/pod-product-compliance
Lightning Source LLC
Chambersburg PA
CBHW072312170526
45158CB00003BA/1286